CW00839535

4 kids to cook	2
savoury	4
sweet	30
glossary	60
conversion chart	62
index	63

contents

Please note that Australian cup and spoon measurements are metric.
A conversion chart appears on page 62.

4 Kids to Cook

Cooking is a great way to get creative and have some fun. Just look at all the yummy treats you can make: cakes, slices, pizza, ice-blocks. But what if you haven't had much experience in the kitchen? It's easy. All you need to learn are a few simple rules and before you know it, your house will have a new master chef – you.

What you will need

Ingredients
Before starting, make sure you have all the ingredients the recipe calls for.

Apron
This will help shield you from food stains, hot oil splashes and provides a place to wipe wet or dirty hands.

Clean hands + work area
Clean hands and work area are a must when cooking. Bacteria can easily be transferred to food, passing germs to family and friends. Wash down the work bench and your hands before you start cooking and after you have finished. Keeping the work area clean during cooking reduces the risk of fire, and an uncluttered work area stops food from accidentally falling onto the floor.

An adult
Adults are handy to have around when cooking. They can let you know about tricky ingredients and can step in when you have to use sharp knives. They also provide an extra set of hands when there is a lot of stirring or chopping to be done. But most of all, cooking is much more fun if you have someone around to help and talk to.

A knife
Most recipes require a knife, so make sure you have one handy. When using sharp knives remember to have an adult to supervise or to step in and help you with anything that needs cutting.

Cooking utensils
Make sure you have all the utensils required for the recipe. Depending on the recipe, you may need bowls, spoons, a grater, spatula, baking trays and tins, measuring cups and spoons, oven mitts, electric beater, saucepans and a chopping board.

Mixers/beaters
These machines are just the thing when beating cake batter, cookie mix or any other type of heavy mixing. They save time so you don't have to stir for too

long, and as a treat you get to lick the beaters after you're done.

Oven and other hot equipment

Make sure an adult is around whenever you are using something hot. Depending on what you are cooking you may need to use the microwave, a grill, toaster, oven or stovetop. Check the recipe for the recommended temperature, cooking time and cooking appliance. Some things will cook very differently in the microwave than they will in the oven.

Tip Set the oven temperature when you are beginning to cook instead of when you need to put the food in the oven. This will give it time to reach the correct temperature.

General rules

• Always read the whole recipe before starting to cook. Check you have all the ingredients, utensils and the time to make the recipe. Some recipes need additional time for standing, refrigeration or freezing.

• Take care with sharp knives and hot surfaces and appliances.

• Always make sure saucepan handles are turned toward the wall to prevent spills and scalds.

• Never put a spoon back in the bowl after licking it.

• Always have clean hands and a clean work area.

chicken quesadilla

2 large flour tortillas
40g packaged reduced-fat cream cheese
½ cup (80g) shredded barbecued chicken
¼ cup (35g) coarsely chopped drained semi-dried tomatoes
½ medium avocado (125g), mashed

1 Place one tortilla on cutting board; spread with cream cheese then top with chicken and tomato.
2 Spread second tortilla with avocado; place tortilla, avocado-side down, on top of first tortilla.
3 Toast in sandwich press until golden brown. Serve quesadilla cut into quarters.

preparation time 5 minutes
cooking time 5 minutes
serves 1
nutritional count per serving 41.2g total fat (11.6g saturated fat); 3265kJ (781 cal); 61.8g carbohydrate; 36.5g protein; 9.1g fibre

mexican bagels

1 bagel
1 tablespoon bottled tomato salsa
½ small avocado (100g), sliced thickly
2 slices cheddar cheese

1 Preheat grill.
2 Split bagel in half horizontally; spread 2 teaspoons of salsa over each bagel half. Top each half with avocado and one cheese slice.
3 Place under grill about 5 minutes or until cheese melts.

preparation time 5 minutes
cooking time 5 minutes
serves 2
nutritional count per bagel half 15.6g total fat (6.1g saturated fat); 1354kJ (324 cal); 32.3g carbohydrate; 12.3g protein; 2.6g fibre
note Try spreading ripe and creamy avocado on your sandwiches instead of butter. Unripe avocados will soften and be ready to eat sooner if they are kept at room temperature rather than in the refrigerator.

cheese twists

2 sheets ready-rolled puff pastry
1 tablespoon tomato sauce
1 cup (100g) pizza cheese
1 tablespoon milk

1 Preheat oven to 220°C/200°C fan-forced. Line oven trays with baking paper.
2 Spread one piece of pastry with sauce; sprinkle with cheese. Top with remaining pastry; press down firmly.
3 Cut pastry into 20 strips. Twist strips, place 2cm apart on trays; brush with milk.
4 Bake about 10 minutes or until browned lightly. Serve warm or at room temperature.

preparation time 15 minutes
cooking time 10 minutes
makes 20
nutritional count per twist 4.9g total fat (2.8g saturated fat); 330kJ (79 cal); 6.3g carbohydrate; 2.4g protein; 0.2g fibre
tips Twists can be cooked up to two days ahead; store in an airtight container. Serve twists at room temperature or reheat, in a single layer, on oven trays, covered loosely with foil, in oven (180°C/160°C fan-forced) for about 10 minutes.
Uncooked twists can be frozen between layers of freezer wrap for up to three months. Cook twists from frozen state, as per recipe.

bruschetta fingers

1 small turkish bread roll (165g)
2 teaspoons sun-dried tomato pesto
6 cherry tomatoes (60g), quartered
30g cherry bocconcini cheese, halved
1 tablespoon finely chopped fresh flat-leaf parsley

1 Split bread in half; toast, cut-side up, then cut into fingers.
2 Spread toasted sides with pesto; top with tomato and cheese then sprinkle with parsley.

preparation time 5 minutes
cooking time 2 minutes
serves 1
nutritional count per serving 12.2g total fat (4.4g saturated fat); 1618kJ (387 cal); 50.6g carbohydrate; 16.3g protein; 4.3g fibre

bacon and corn pizza

1 pocket pitta bread (85g)
1 tablespoon corn relish
1 rindless bacon rasher (65g), chopped finely
2 tablespoons pizza cheese
1 tablespoon coarsely chopped fresh flat-leaf parsley

1 Preheat oven to 180°C/160°C fan-forced.
2 Spread bread with relish. Place on oven tray; top with bacon and cheese. Cook, uncovered, about 15 minutes or until bacon crisps and cheese melts. Sprinkle parsley over pizza just before serving.

preparation time 5 minutes
cooking time 15 minutes
serves 1
nutritional count per serving 17.3g total fat (7.7g saturated fat); 2027kJ (485 cal); 50.5g carbohydrate; 29.7g protein; 3g fibre

mini pizzas

4 pitta pocket breads (340g)
⅓ cup (90g) tomato paste
150g cabanossi, sliced thinly
100g ham, chopped finely
½ medium red capsicum (100g), chopped finely
440g can pineapple pieces in natural juice, drained
1½ cups (180g) grated cheddar cheese

1 Preheat oven to 220°C/200°C fan-forced.
2 Spread each pocket bread with 1 tablespoon of the tomato paste.
3 Place pocket breads on oven trays; top with cabanossi, ham, capsicum and pineapple. Sprinkle with cheese.
4 Cook, uncovered, about 12 minutes or until cheese melts and is browned lightly.

preparation time 10 minutes
cooking time 10 minutes
makes 4
nutritional count per pizza 27.4g total fat (14g saturated fat); 2554kJ (611 cal); 56.9g carbohydrate; 31.3g protein; 5g fibre
tip Don't assemble the pizzas until you are ready to cook them.

mini pizza torpedoes

12 "bake at home" bread rolls
½ cup (130g) tomato pasta sauce
1½ cups (180g) coarsely grated cheddar cheese
5 slices (25g) mild salami, chopped coarsely
10 seeded black olives, chopped finely
3 green onions, chopped finely
100g leg ham, chopped finely
⅓ cup drained canned crushed pineapple

1 Preheat oven to 200°C/180°C fan-forced.
2 Cut each roll in half lengthways. Place rolls on oven tray, cut-side-up; spread each half with sauce. Sprinkle half the cheese over rolls.
3 Sprinkle 12 roll halves with salami, olives and half the onion. Sprinkle remaining rolls with ham, pineapple and remaining onion.
4 Sprinkle remaining cheese over tops of rolls.
5 Bake about 10 minutes or until cheese has melted.

preparation time 15 minutes
cooking time 10 minutes
serves 12
nutritional count per serving 8.9g total fat (4g saturated fat);
1246kJ (298 cal); 39.8g carbohydrate; 12.6g protein; 3.3g fibre

sausage rolls

2 teaspoons vegetable oil

1 small brown onion (80g), grated coarsely

1 slice stale white bread, crusts removed

200g sausage mince

200g beef mince

2 teaspoons tomato paste

½ teaspoon dried mixed herbs

1 tablespoon finely chopped fresh flat-leaf parsley

2 sheets ready-rolled puff pastry

1 egg, beaten lightly

1 Preheat oven to 220°C/200°C fan-forced. Line two oven trays with baking paper.

2 Heat oil in small frying pan; cook onion until soft.

3 Dip bread quickly in and out of a small bowl of cold water; discard water.

4 Combine onion and bread in medium bowl with minces, paste, dried herbs and parsley.

5 Cut pastry sheets in half lengthways. Spoon mixture along centre of each pastry piece. Turn one long side of pastry over mince mixture; brush pastry flap with egg. Turn other long side of pastry over to enclose mince mixture.

6 Cut each roll into six pieces. Place rolls, seam-side down, on trays; brush with egg. Make two cuts in top of each roll; bake rolls about 30 minutes or until browned.

7 Stand 10 minutes before serving with tomato sauce.

preparation time 15 minutes
cooking time 30 minutes
makes 24
nutritional count per roll 6.5g total fat (3.1g saturated fat);410kJ (98 cal); 5.8g carbohydrate; 3.9g protein; 0.5g fibre
tips Uncooked rolls can be frozen between layers of freezer wrap for up to three months; wrap uncut rolls individually in plastic (we used the plastic that separates the pastry sheets) and freeze in an airtight container for up to three months. Thaw uncut rolls in refrigerator for about 12 hours or overnight. Cut and bake as per recipe.

vegetable rice paper rolls

1 large carrot (180g), grated coarsely
2 trimmed celery stalks (200g), chopped finely
150g wombok, shredded finely
2 teaspoons fish sauce
2 teaspoons brown sugar
1 tablespoon lemon juice
24 x 17cm-square rice paper sheets
24 fresh mint leaves

1 Combine carrot, celery, wombok, sauce, sugar and juice in medium bowl.
2 Place 1 sheet of rice paper in medium bowl of warm water until just softened; lift sheet carefully from water, place on tea-towel covered chopping board.
3 Place 1 level tablespoon of vegetable mixture across edge of sheet; top with mint leaf. Roll to enclose filling, folding in ends. Repeat with remaining rice paper sheets, vegetable mixture and mint leaves.
4 Serve with sweet chilli sauce, if desired.

preparation time 30 minutes
makes 24
nutritional count per roll 0.2g total fat (0g saturated fat); 92kJ (22 cal); 3.9g carbohydrate; 0.8g protein; 0.7g fibre
tip Rolls can be made three hours ahead; cover with a slightly damp cloth then foil or plastic wrap, and keep in the refrigerator.

oven-baked fish 'n' chips
with tartare sauce

1kg potatoes, peeled
cooking-oil spray
8 firm white fish fillets (960g)
¼ cup (35g) plain flour
3 egg whites, beaten lightly
1 tablespoon milk
2¼ cups (155g) stale
    breadcrumbs
¾ cup (120g) cornflake crumbs
tartare sauce
2 egg yolks
1 tablespoon lemon juice
½ teaspoon mustard powder
1 cup (250ml) vegetable oil
2 tablespoons milk,
    approximately
2 tablespoons finely chopped
    gherkins
2 tablespoons rinsed drained
    capers, chopped finely
2 tablespoons finely chopped
    fresh chives

1 Preheat oven to 200°C/180°C fan-forced.
2 Cut potatoes into 1.5cm slices; cut slices into 1cm chips. Place chips, in single layer, on oiled oven trays; spray lightly with oil. Bake, uncovered, about 35 minutes or until brown.
3 Meanwhile, working with one fish fillet at a time, toss fish in flour, shake off excess; dip fish into combined egg white and milk, then combined crumbs. Place on oiled oven tray; repeat with remaining fish. Bake fish, uncovered, for the final 20 minutes of chip baking time.
4 Meanwhile, make tartare sauce. Serve fish and chips with tartare sauce.

tartare sauce Blend or process egg yolks, juice and mustard until smooth. With motor operating, gradually add oil, in a thin steady stream; process until sauce thickens. Place in serving bowl; whisk in only enough milk to give desired consistency. Stir in remaining ingredients.

preparation time 35 minutes
cooking time 35 minutes
serves 4
nutritional count per serving 66.1g total fat (9.7g saturated fat); 4753kJ (1137 cal); 88.7g carbohydrate; 43.7g protein; 6.6g fibre
tip Any boneless firm white fish fillet can be used in this recipe: blue eye, bream swordfish, ling, whiting or sea perch are all good choices. Check for any small pieces of bone in the fillets and use tweezers to remove them.

cheeseburgers

500g beef mince
1 medium brown onion (150g),
   grated coarsely
1 teaspoon dried mixed herbs
2 tablespoons barbecue sauce
½ cup (50g) packaged
   breadcrumbs
1 egg, beaten lightly
¼ cup (60ml) olive oil
4 hamburger buns, cut in half
4 lettuce leaves
2 medium egg tomatoes
   (150g), sliced thinly
½ x 450g can sliced beetroot,
   drained
4 slices cheddar cheese
¼ cup (60ml) tomato sauce

1 Combine beef, onion, herbs, barbecue sauce, breadcrumbs and egg in large bowl. Shape mixture into four patties.
2 Heat oil in large frying pan, add patties; cook over medium heat about 15 minutes or until cooked through. Remove patties from pan; drain on absorbent paper.
3 Preheat grill. Toast buns, cut-side up, under grill. Layer bottom half of bun with lettuce, tomato, beetroot, patties, cheese and tomato sauce. Top with remaining bun half.

preparation time 15 minutes
cooking time 15 minutes
serves 4
nutritional count per serving 32.4g total fat (10.2g saturated fat); 2997kJ (717 cal); 60.6g carbohydrate; 43.3g protein; 6.2g fibre
tip Use the best-quality, low-fat beef mince you can find to make these burgers.

pitta filled with lamb and tabouleh

¾ cup (200g) low-fat yogurt
2 cloves garlic, crushed
500g lamb mince
1 teaspoon ground cumin
1 teaspoon ground coriander
½ small brown onion (40g), chopped finely
1 egg
4 pocket pitta breads (340g)
½ baby cos lettuce (90g), leaves separated
⅔ cup (115g) tabbouleh

1 Combine yogurt and half the garlic in small bowl.
2 Combine remaining garlic, mince, spices, onion and egg in medium bowl. Shape into eight patties.
3 Cook patties in heated oiled large frying pan.
4 Split breads not quite through; fill pockets with lettuce, tabbouleh, patties and garlic yogurt.

preparation time 15 minutes
cooking time 15 minutes
serves 4
nutritional count per serving 15.7g total fat (5.2g saturated fat); 2132kJ (510 cal); 49.9g carbohydrate; 39.3g protein; 4.7g fibre

marinated pork ribs

4 slabs (1.5kg) American-style pork ribs
⅓ cup (80ml) plum sauce
2 tablespoons barbecue sauce
2 tablespoons tomato sauce
1 tablespoon soy sauce

1 Place pork in large shallow glass dish, pour over combined sauces; turn pork to coat in marinade. Cover, refrigerate 3 hours or overnight.
2 Preheat oven to 200°C/180°C fan-forced.
3 Remove pork from marinade; reserve marinade. Place pork, in a single layer, on wire rack over baking dish (you might need two dishes).
4 Cook pork, uncovered, 20 minutes. Brush pork with reserved marinade; cook further 20 minutes or until cooked through.

preparation time 5 minutes (plus refrigeration time)
cooking time 40 minutes
serves 4
nutritional count per serving 11.1g total fat (3.6g saturated fat); 1271kJ (304 cal); 22.2g carbohydrate; 29.1g protein; 0.5g fibre
tip A slab of American-style pork spareribs will consist of between 7 and 10 ribs each. After the meat is cooked, get an adult to separate the ribs with a knife, then eat them with your hands.

banana cake

125g butter, softened
¾ cup (165g) firmly packed
brown sugar
2 eggs
1½ cups (225g) self-raising flour
½ teaspoon bicarbonate
of soda
1 teaspoon mixed spice
1 cup mashed banana
½ cup (120g) sour cream
¼ cup (60ml) milk
cream cheese icing
1 cup (160g) icing sugar
250g cream cheese

1 Preheat oven to 180°C/160°C fan-forced.
Grease 15cm x 25cm loaf pan; line base with
baking paper.
2 Beat butter and sugar in small bowl with
electric mixer until light and fluffy. Beat in eggs,
one at a time, until combined. Transfer mixture
to large bowl; using wooden spoon, stir in
sifted dry ingredients, banana, sour cream
and milk. Spread mixture into pan.
3 Bake cake about 50 minutes. Stand cake
5 minutes before turning, top-side up, onto
wire rack to cool.
4 Meanwhile, make cream cheese icing.
5 Spread cold cake with cream cheese icing.
cream cheese icing Beat sifted icing sugar
and cream cheese in small bowl with electric
mixer, on medium speed, until mixture is smooth.

preparation time 35 minutes (plus cooling time)
cooking time 55 minutes
serves 10
nutritional count per serving 24.9g total fat
(15.7g saturated fat); 1898kJ (454 cal);
52.4g carbohydrate; 6.7g protein; 1.4g fibre
tips You need two large overripe bananas for
this recipe. If the bananas you buy are not ripe
enough, put them in a paper bag and keep
them at room temperature for a day or two.

gingerbread biscuits

125g butter, chopped
⅓ cup (75g) firmly packed
    brown sugar
½ cup (175g) golden syrup
3 cups (450g) plain flour
2 teaspoons ground ginger
2 teaspoons ground cinnamon
½ teaspoon ground clove
2 teaspoons bicarbonate
    of soda
1 egg, beaten lightly
1 teaspoon vanilla extract
sparkling cachous, to decorate
royal icing
2 egg whites
3 cups (480g) pure icing sugar
food colourings

1 Preheat oven to 180°C/160°C fan-forced.
Grease and line oven trays with baking paper.
2 Combine butter, sugar and golden syrup
in small saucepan; stir over low heat until
smooth. Cool 5 minutes.
3 Sift flour, spices and soda into large bowl;
add butter mixture, egg and extract, stir until
mixture is combined.
4 Knead dough on floured surface until smooth.
Roll dough between sheets of baking paper to
5mm thickness; refrigerate 10 minutes.
5 Using round, heart and star-shaped cutters,
cut out shapes from dough; place on trays.
6 Bake about 10 minutes or until browned.
Cool on trays.
7 Meanwhile, make royal icing.
8 Decorate biscuits by spreading or piping
with royal icing; decorate with cachous.
royal icing Beat egg whites in small bowl with
electric mixer until frothy; gradually beat in
sifted icing sugar, a tablespoon at a time, until
stiff peaks form. Tint icing as desired. Keep
icing covered with a damp cloth, or enclosed
tightly in plastic piping bags; the icing will
develop a crust once it's exposed to the air.

tips To make a quick piping
bag, snip off a corner of a
small plastic bag.
Un-iced biscuits can be made
three days ahead; store in
an airtight container. Freeze
un-iced biscuits between layers
of freezer wrap for up to one
month. Thaw biscuits at room
temperature for one hour.

preparation time 30 minutes
cooking time 10 minutes
makes 20
nutritional count per biscuit 5.7g total fat
(3.5g saturated fat); 1124kJ (269 cal);
50.4g carbohydrate; 3.2g protein; 0.9g fibre

yogurt, berry and
white chocolate muffins

1½ cups (240g) wholemeal self-raising flour
½ cup (110g) caster sugar
2 tablespoons vegetable oil
2 eggs, beaten lightly
1 cup (280g) low-fat yogurt
1 cup (150g) frozen mixed berries
100g white eating chocolate, chopped coarsely

1 Preheat oven to 180°C/160°C fan-forced. Grease 12-hole
(⅓-cup/80ml) muffin pan.
2 Combine flour and sugar in large bowl. Add remaining ingredients;
mix batter until just combined. Divide batter among pan holes; bake
about 30 minutes.
3 Stand muffins 5 minutes before serving; dust with sifted icing sugar,
if you like.

preparation time 10 minutes
cooking time 25 minutes
makes 12
nutritional count per muffin 7.2g total fat (2.5g saturated fat);
807kJ (193 cal); 25.3g carbohydrate; 5.6g protein; 2.4g fibre
tips You can use milk or dark chocolate instead of the white chocolate
for the muffins and still get the same melt-in-the-mouth result. These
muffins are best served warm.

berry muffins

2½ cups (375g) self-raising flour
90g cold butter, chopped
1 cup (220g) caster sugar
1¼ cups (310ml) buttermilk
1 egg, beaten lightly
200g fresh or frozen mixed berries

1 Preheat oven to 180°C/160°C fan-forced. Grease 12-hole
(⅓-cup/80ml) muffin pan.
2 Sift flour into large bowl; using fingertips, rub in butter. Stir in sugar,
buttermilk and egg. Do not over-mix; mixture should be lumpy. Add
berries; stir through gently.
3 Spoon mixture into pan holes; bake about 20 minutes. Stand muffins
5 minutes; turn, top-side up, onto wire rack to cool.

preparation time 10 minutes
cooking time 20 minutes
makes 12
nutritional count per muffin 7.5g total fat (4.6g saturated fat);
1095kJ (262 cal); 42.4g carbohydrate; 5.1g protein; 1.6g fibre
tip Muffins can be stored in an airtight container for up to two days.

variations
lemon poppy seed Omit berries. Add 2 teaspoons lemon rind and
2 tablespoons poppy seeds with the sugar.
date and orange Omit berries. Substitute self-raising flour with
1 cup wholemeal self-raising flour and 1½ cups white self-raising flour.
Add 1½ cups seeded, chopped dried dates and 2 teaspoons finely
grated orange rind with the sugar.
choc-chip and walnut Omit mixed berries. Add ¾ cup dark Choc Bits
and 1 cup coarsely chopped walnuts with the sugar.

patty cakes with glace icing

125g butter, softened
1 teaspoon vanilla extract
⅔ cup (150g) caster sugar
3 eggs
1½ cups (225g) self-raising flour
¼ cup (60ml) milk
glace icing
1½ cups (240g) icing sugar
1 teaspoon butter, softened
2 tablespoons milk,
    approximately

1 Preheat oven to 180°C/160°C fan-forced. Line two deep 12-hole patty pans with paper cases.

2 Combine ingredients in medium bowl; beat on low speed with electric mixer until ingredients are combined. Increase speed to medium; beat about 3 minutes or until mixture is smooth and paler in colour.

3 Drop rounded tablespoons of mixture into paper cases. Bake about 20 minutes. Stand cakes in pans 5 minutes before turning, top-side up, onto wire racks to cool.

4 Make glace icing.

5 Top cold cakes with glace icing.

glace icing Sift icing sugar into small heatproof bowl; stir in butter and enough milk to give a firm paste. Set bowl over small saucepan of simmering water; stir until icing is spreadable.

preparation time 15 minutes (plus cooling time)
cooking time 25 minutes
makes 24
nutritional count per cake 5.4g total fat (3.2g saturated fat); 627kJ (150 cal); 23.1g carbohydrate; 1.9g protein; 0.4g fibre
tips Cakes can be stored in an airtight container, at room temperature, for two days. Uniced cakes can be frozen for two months.

buttermilk scones

3 cups (450g) self-raising flour
1 teaspoon icing sugar
60g butter, chopped
1¾ cups (430ml) buttermilk
300ml thickened cream
¾ cup (240g) strawberry jam

1 Preheat oven to 220°C/200°C fan-forced. Grease and flour 23cm-square cake pan.

2 Combine flour, icing sugar and butter in food processor; process until mixture resembles breadcrumbs. Add buttermilk; process until just combined (mixture should be sticky). Turn dough onto floured surface, knead lightly until smooth.

3 Press dough out into 3cm thickness. Using a 5.5cm round cutter, cut dough into 16 rounds. (You will need to gently re-roll the dough to get the 16 rounds.)

4 Place scones into pan; they should fit comfortably, just touching one another slightly. Bake, uncovered, about 20 minutes or until browned lightly.

5 Meanwhile, beat cream in small bowl with electric mixer until thickened.

6 Serve warm scones, cut in half, topped with jam and cream.

preparation time 15 minutes
cooking time 20 minutes
makes 16
nutritional count per half scone with jam and cream 10.9g total fat (7g saturated fat); 978kJ (234 cal); 29.1g carbohydrate; 4.4g protein; 1.2g fibre
tip Scones should be browned and sound hollow when tapped firmly on the top with your fingers. The scones in the middle are the ones to tap, they will take the longest to cook.

chewy chocolate slice

125g butter, melted
1 cup (220g) firmly packed brown sugar
1 egg
1 teaspoon vanilla extract
½ cup (75g) plain flour
¼ cup (35g) self-raising flour
2 tablespoons cocoa powder
½ cup (40g) desiccated coconut
1 tablespoon shredded coconut
chocolate icing
1 cup (160g) icing sugar
2 tablespoons cocoa powder
10g butter
1 tablespoon hot water

1 Preheat oven to 180°C/160°C fan-forced. Grease 19cm x 29cm slice pan; line base and two long sides with baking paper, extending paper 5cm above edges.
2 Combine butter, sugar, egg and extract in medium bowl. Stir in sifted flours and cocoa then desiccated coconut.
3 Spread mixture over base of pan. Bake about 25 minutes or until firm.
4 Meanwhile, make chocolate icing.
5 Spread hot slice with chocolate icing; sprinkle with shredded coconut, cool. When cool, cut slice into 15 squares; cut squares into triangles.
chocolate icing Sift icing sugar and cocoa into small bowl; add butter and the water, stir until smooth.

preparation time 15 minutes (plus cooling time)
cooking time 25 minutes
makes 30
nutritional count per piece 5g total fat (3.5g saturated fat); 468kJ (112 cal); 15.4g carbohydrate; 0.9g protein; 0.4g fibre
tip Slice can be made one week ahead; store in an airtight container at room temperature.

sweet

triple-choc brownies

125g butter, chopped
200g dark eating chocolate, chopped coarsely
½ cup (110g) caster sugar
2 eggs
1¼ cups (185g) plain flour
150g white eating chocolate, chopped coarsely
100g milk eating chocolate, chopped coarsely

1 Preheat oven to 180°C/160°C fan-forced. Grease deep
19cm-square cake pan; line base and sides with baking paper,
extending paper 5cm over sides.
2 Combine butter and dark chocolate in medium saucepan; stir
over low heat until smooth. Cool 10 minutes.
3 Stir in sugar and eggs then sifted flour and white and milk chocolates.
Spread mixture into pan. Bake about 35 minutes. Cool in pan before
turning out and cutting into squares.

preparation time 20 minutes
cooking time 40 minutes
makes 16
nutritional count per brownie 15.6g total fat (9.6g saturated fat);
1191kJ (285 cal); 32.1g carbohydrate; 4g protein; 0.6g fibre
tip Brownies can be stored, in an airtight container, in the refrigerator,
for up to four days.

chocolate-dipped fruit pieces

2 medium bananas (400g), sliced thickly
250g strawberries
3 apricots (150g), quartered
1¼ cups (185g) milk chocolate Melts, melted

1 Line tray with baking paper.
2 Dip fruit, one piece at a time, into chocolate to coat about half of each piece of fruit. Place fruit, in single layer, on tray; allow to set at room temperature.

preparation time 15 minutes (plus standing time)
makes 30
nutritional count per piece 2g total fat (1.2g saturated fat); 196kJ (47 cal); 6.2g carbohydrate; 0.7g protein; 0.6g fibre
tip Fruit is best dipped on the day of serving. If weather is hot, refrigerate dipped fruit.

sweet

white chocolate rocky road

½ cup (150g) raspberry lollies, chopped coarsely
2 tablespoons desiccated coconut
100g packet mallow bakes
375g white chocolate Melts, melted

1 Line two 12-hole (1-tablespoon/20ml) mini muffin pans with paper cases.
2 Combine raspberries, coconut and mallow bakes in medium bowl.
3 Pour chocolate into small plastic bag; snip corner to make piping bag.
Pipe enough chocolate into each case to cover base.
4 Press raspberry mixture into paper cases. Pipe remaining chocolate over
raspberry mixture. Refrigerate until chocolate has set.

preparation time 15 minutes (plus refrigeration time)
makes 24
nutritional count per piece 5.5g total fat (3.6g saturated fat);
501kJ (120 cal); 15.9g carbohydrate; 1.7g protein; 0.1g fibre
tip Rocky road can be made one week ahead; store in an airtight container.
Store in the refrigerator if weather is hot.

vanilla-caramel swirl
ice-cream blocks

1½ cups softened vanilla ice-cream
¼ cup (60ml) caramel-flavoured topping

1   Spoon ice-cream into six ¼-cup (60ml) ice-block moulds.
2   Swirl 2 teaspoons topping into each mould. Press lids on firmly;
freeze 6 hours or overnight.

preparation time 5 minutes (plus freezing time)
makes 6
nutritional count per block   2.7g total fat (1.9g saturated fat);
322kJ (77 cal); 12.5g carbohydrate; 1.2g protein; 0.1g fibre

sweet

chocolate sundaes

2 litres vanilla ice-cream
100g marshmallows
½ cup (70g) crushed nuts
12 ice-cream wafers
hot chocolate sauce
200g dark eating chocolate, chopped coarsely
½ cup (125ml) thickened cream

1 Make hot chocolate sauce.
2 Place a little of the hot chocolate sauce in the bottom of six
¾-cup (180ml) serving glasses; top with ice-cream, marshmallows,
more chocolate sauce, nuts and wafer biscuits.
hot chocolate sauce Combine chocolate and cream in small
saucepan; stir over low heat until chocolate is melted and sauce
is smooth, do not overheat.

preparation time 5 minutes
cooking time 5 minutes
serves 6
nutritional count per serving 41.1g total fat (26.7g saturated fat);
2826kJ (676 cal); 70.3g carbohydrate; 11.4g protein; 2.5g fibre
tip Make quick banana splits by slicing half a banana over the top
of each sundae.

chocolate mousse

200g dark eating chocolate, chopped coarsely
30g unsalted butter
3 eggs, separated
300ml thickened cream, whipped

1 Melt chocolate in medium heatproof bowl over medium saucepan of simmering water. Remove from heat; add butter, stir until smooth. Stir in egg yolks. Transfer mixture to large bowl, cover; cool.
2 Beat egg whites in small bowl with electric mixer until soft peaks form. Fold egg whites and cream into chocolate mixture, in two batches.
3 Divide mousse among serving dishes; refrigerate 3 hours or overnight. Serve with extra whipped cream, chocolate curls and fresh raspberries, if desired.

preparation time 20 minutes (plus cooling and refrigeration time)
cooking time 5 minutes
serves 6
nutritional count per serving 34.9g total fat (21.4g saturated fat); 1777kJ (425 cal); 22.5g carbohydrate; 6.1g protein; 0.4g fibre
tips Store mousse, covered, in the refrigerator for up to two days. To make chocolate curls, run a vegetable peeler down the side of a block of dark eating chocolate.

snakes-alive jelly cups

2 x 85g packets green jelly crystals
12 large jelly snakes
85g packet yellow jelly crystals

1 Make green jelly according to directions on packets; cool. Pour jelly evenly among 12 x ⅔-cup (160ml) clear plastic cups.
2 Curl one snake into each cup of jelly, with snake's head hanging over edge of cup. Refrigerate about 3 hours or until jelly is set.
3 Make yellow jelly according to directions on packet; cool. Carefully pour yellow jelly over green jelly in cups; refrigerate about 3 hours or until set.

preparation time 15 minutes (plus refrigeration time)
makes 12
nutritional count per serving 0g total fat (0g saturated fat); 568kJ (136 cal); 30.9g carbohydrate; 2.6g protein; 0g fibre
tip Jelly cups can be made one day ahead of serving.

banana pancakes

½ cup (75g) self-raising flour
1 tablespoon caster sugar
⅔ cup (160ml) buttermilk
1 egg white
2 tablespoons maple syrup
10g butter, melted
1 medium banana (200g), sliced thinly
¼ cup (60ml) maple syrup, extra
¼ cup (30g) roasted pecans, chopped coarsely

1 Combine sifted flour and sugar in medium bowl; whisk in buttermilk, egg white, syrup and butter until mixture is smooth. Stir in banana.
2 Pour ¼ cup of the batter into heated oiled large frying pan. Cook, uncovered, until bubbles appear on surface. Turn; cook until browned lightly. Remove from pan; cover to keep warm. Repeat process with remaining batter to make a total of eight pancakes.
3 Serve pancakes drizzled with extra syrup then sprinkled with nuts.

preparation time 10 minutes
cooking time 10 minutes
serves 4
nutritional count per serving 8.6g total fat (2.3g saturated fat); 1271kJ (304 cal); 49.4g carbohydrate; 5.7g protein; 2.1g fibre

glossary

american-style pork ribs
trimmed pork mid-loin ribs.

bicarbonate of soda also
known as baking soda or
carb soda.

bread

bagel small ring-shaped
bread roll; yeast-based but
egg-less, with a dense,
chewy texture and shiny
crust. A true bagel is boiled
in water before it's baked.

bake at home rolls partially-
baked bread only needing a
few minutes in the oven to
give fresh-baked rolls.

pitta also known as lebanese
bread. A wheat-flour pocket
bread sold in large, flat pieces
that separate into two thin
rounds. Also available in
small thick pieces called
pocket pitta.

pide also known as turkish
bread. Comes in long (about
45cm) flat loaves as well as
individual rounds.

breadcrumbs

packaged fine-textured,
crunchy, purchased white
breadcrumbs.

stale one- or two-day-old
bread made into crumbs by
blending or processing.

buttermilk sold alongside
all fresh milk products in
supermarkets; slightly sour
liquid left after butter was
churned from cream. Despite
its name, it is low in fat.

cabanossi a processed
sausage made from pork,
beef, spices and garlic.

cachous also known as
dragées; tiny (3-5mm) edible,
metallic-looking confectionery
balls used in cake decorating;
available in silver, gold or
various colours.

capers the grey-green buds
of a warm climate (usually
Mediterranean) shrub, sold
either dried and salted, or
pickled in a vinegar brine.
Baby capers are smaller,
and fuller-flavoured. Rinse
well before using.

capsicum also known
as bell pepper or, simply,
pepper. Can be red, green,
yellow, orange or purplish-
black in colour. Discard seeds
and membranes before use.

cheese

bocconcini a delicate, white,
semi-soft cheese. A smaller
version of mozzarella.

cream cheese a soft cow-
milk cheese; also known
as Philadelphia or Philly.

pizza a blend of grated
mozzarella, cheddar and
parmesan cheeses.

chocolate

chocolate Melts ideal for
melting and moulding.

dark eating also known
as semi-sweet or luxury
chocolate; made of a high
percentage of cocoa liquor
and cocoa butter, and a
little added sugar.

milk eating most popular
eating chocolate; mild and
very sweet, similar in make-
up to dark eating chocolate.

white eating contains no
cocoa solids; its sweetness
comes from cocoa butter.

cocoa powder also known
as cocoa; dried, roasted
then ground cocoa beans.

coconut

desiccated unsweetened,
concentrated, dried, finely
shredded coconut.

shredded thin strips of
dried coconut.

corn relish a cooked or
pickled sauce made with
corn and spices and used
as a condiment.

corn flake crumbs packaged
crumbs made from crushed
corn flakes.

cos lettuce also known as
romaine lettuce. Long, with
leaves ranging from dark
green on the outside to
almost white near the core.

fish fillets, firm white any
boneless firm white fish fillet
can be used – blue eye,
bream, swordfish, ling,
whiting or sea perch are
all good choices. Check for
any small pieces of bone in
the fillets and use tweezers
to remove them.

flat-leaf parsley also known
as continental parsley or
italian parsley.

flour

plain an all-purpose flour
made from wheat.

self-raising plain flour sifted
with baking powder in the
proportion of 1 cup flour to
2 teaspoons baking powder.

wholemeal also known as whole wheat flour; milled with the wheat germ so is higher in fibre and more nutritional than plain flour.

gherkin the young fruit of a small variety of dark green cucumbers grown for pickling.

golden syrup a by-product of refined sugar cane; pure maple syrup or honey can be substituted.

jelly crystals also known as jello; a powdered mixture of gelatine, sweetener and artificial fruit flavouring.

maple syrup a thin syrup distilled from the sap of the maple tree. Maple-flavoured syrup or pancake syrup is not an adequate substitute for the real thing.

mince meat also known as ground meat.

mustard powder finely ground white (yellow) mustard seeds.

oil
cooking-oil spray we used a canola-oil spray.
olive made from olives.
vegetable sourced from plants rather than animal fats.

ready-rolled puff pastry packaged sheets of frozen puff pastry available from supermarkets.

rice paper sheets also known as banh trang. Made from rice paste and stamped into rounds; when dipped into warm water, becomes a pliable wrapper for food.

salami cured (air-dried) sausages heavily seasoned with garlic and spices.

sauce
fish also called nam pla or nuoc nam; made from pulverised salted fermented fish, most often anchovies. Has a pungent smell and strong taste, so use sparingly.
plum a thick, sweet and sour dipping sauce made from plums, vinegar, sugar, chillies and spices.
soy made from fermented soy beans. Several variations are available in Asian food stores and supermarkets. We use japanese soy sauce unless otherwise indicated.

pasta, bottled tomato a blend of tomatoes, herbs and spices.

sour cream a thick, cultured soured cream.

spices
ground cinnamon dried inner bark of the shoots of the cinnamon tree.
ground clove dried flower buds of a tropical tree. They have a strong scent and taste, so use sparingly.
ground coriander ground coriander seeds; must not replace fresh coriander, or vice versa, as the tastes are completely different.
ground cumin also known as zeera or comino; has a spicy, nutty flavour.
ground ginger also known as powdered ginger.

mixed spice a blend of ground spices usually consisting of cinnamon, allspice and nutmeg.

sugar
caster also known as finely granulated or superfine table sugar.
icing sugar also known as confectioners' sugar or powdered sugar; granulated sugar crushed together with a small amount of cornflour.
pure icing also known as confectioners' sugar or powdered sugar (has no added cornflour).

tabbouleh a Middle-Eastern dish made with burghul, parsley, tomatoes, cucumber and mint.

tomato
paste triple-concentrated tomato puree.
pesto, sun-dried made from sun-dried tomatoes, oil, vinegar and herbs – a thick tomato paste.
semi-dried partially dried tomato pieces in olive oil. Soft and juicy in texture.

vanilla extract obtained from vanilla beans infused in water; a non-alcoholic version of essence.

wombok also known as peking or chinese cabbage or petsai; elongated with pale green, crinkly leaves. Most popular cabbage in South-East Asia. Available from Asian grocery stores and supermarkets.

conversion chart

MEASURES

One Australian metric measuring cup holds approximately 250ml, one Australian metric tablespoon holds 20ml, one Australian metric teaspoon holds 5ml.

The difference between one country's measuring cups and another's is within a 2- or 3-teaspoon variance, and will not affect your cooking results. North America, New Zealand and the United Kingdom use a 15ml tablespoon. All cup and spoon measurements are level. The most accurate way of measuring dry ingredients is to weigh them. When measuring liquids, use a clear glass or plastic jug with metric markings.

We use large eggs with an average weight of 60g.

DRY MEASURES

METRIC	IMPERIAL
15g	½oz
30g	1oz
60g	2oz
90g	3oz
125g	4oz (¼lb)
155g	5oz
185g	6oz
220g	7oz
250g	8oz (½lb)
280g	9oz
315g	10oz
345g	11oz
375g	12oz (¾lb)
410g	13oz
440g	14oz
470g	15oz
500g	16oz (1lb)
750g	24oz (1½lb)
1kg	32oz (2lb)

LIQUID MEASURES

METRIC	IMPERIAL
30ml	1 fluid oz
60ml	2 fluid oz
100ml	3 fluid oz
125ml	4 fluid oz
150ml	5 fluid oz (¼ pint/1 gill)
190ml	6 fluid oz
250ml	8 fluid oz
300ml	10 fluid oz (½ pint)
500ml	16 fluid oz
600ml	20 fluid oz (1 pint)
1000ml (1 litre)	1¾ pints

LENGTH MEASURES

METRIC	IMPERIAL
3mm	⅛in
6mm	¼in
1cm	½in
2cm	¾in
2.5cm	1in
5cm	2in
6cm	2½in
8cm	3in
10cm	4in
13cm	5in
15cm	6in
18cm	7in
20cm	8in
23cm	9in
25cm	10in
28cm	11in
30cm	12in (1ft)

OVEN TEMPERATURES

These oven temperatures are only a guide for conventional ovens. For fan-forced ovens, check the manufacturer's manual.

	°C (CELSIUS)	°F (FAHRENHEIT)	GAS MARK
Very slow	120	250	½
Slow	150	275-300	1-2
Moderately slow	160	325	3
Moderate	180	350-375	4-5
Moderately hot	200	400	6
Hot	220	425-450	7-8
Very hot	240	475	9

index

B
bacon and corn pizza 12
bagels, mexican 7
banana cake 31
banana pancakes 59
berry muffins 36
biscuits, gingerbread 32
brownies, triple-choc 44
bruschetta fingers 11
buttermilk scones 40

C
cake, banana 31
cakes, patty 39
cheese twists 8
cheeseburgers 24
chewy chocolate slice 43
chicken quesadilla 4
chips 'n' fish, oven-baked 23
choc-chip and
  walnut muffins 36
chocolate
  choc-chip and walnut
    muffins 36
  icing 43
  mousse 55
  slice, chewy 43
  sundaes 52
  triple-choc brownies 44
  white, rocky road 48
  white, yogurt and
    berry muffins 35
  dipped fruit pieces 47
cream cheese icing 31

D
date and orange muffins 36

F
fish 'n' chips, oven-baked 23

fruit pieces,
  chocolate-dipped 47

G
gingerbread biscuits 32
glace icing 39

I
ice-cream blocks, vanilla-
  caramel swirl 51
icings
  royal 32
  chocolate 43
  cream cheese 31
  glace 39

J
jelly cups, snakes-alive 56

L
lamb and tabouleh,
  pitta filled 27
lemon poppy seed muffins 36

M
marinated pork ribs 28
mexican bagels 7
mini pizza torpedoes 16
mini pizzas 15
mousse, chocolate 55
muffins
  berry 36
  choc-chip and walnut 36
  date and orange 36
  lemon poppy seed 36
  yogurt, berry and white
    chocolate muffins 35

O
orange and date muffins 36
oven-baked fish 'n' chips 23

P
pancakes, banana 59
patty cakes 39
pitta filled with lamb
  and tabouleh 27
pizza torpedoes, mini 16
pizza, bacon and corn 12
pizzas, mini 15
pork ribs, marinated 28

Q
quesadilla, chicken 4

R
rocky road, white chocolate 48
rolls, sausage 19
rolls, vegetable rice paper 20
royal icing 32

S
sauce, tartare 23
sausage rolls 19
scones, buttermilk 40
slice, chewy chocolate 43
snakes-alive jelly cups 56
sundaes, chocolate 52

T
tartare sauce 23
triple-choc brownies 44

V
vanilla-caramel swirl
  ice-cream blocks 51
vegetable rice paper rolls 20

W
walnut and choc-chip
  muffins 36
white chocolate rocky road 48
white chocolate, yogurt and
  berry muffins 35

Are you missing some of the world's favourite cookbooks?

The Australian Women's Weekly cookbooks are available from bookshops, cookshops, supermarkets and other stores all over the world. You can also buy direct from the publisher, using the order form below.

MINI SERIES £3.50 190x138MM 64 PAGES

TITLE	QTY	TITLE	QTY	TITLE	QTY
4 Fast Ingredients		Grills & Barbecues		Quick Desserts	
4 Kids to Cook		Healthy Everyday Food 4 Kids		Roast	
15-minute Feasts		Ice-creams & Sorbets		Salads	
50 Fast Chicken Fillets		Indian Cooking		Simple Slices	
50 Fast Desserts		Indonesian Favourites		Simply Seafood	
Barbecue Chicken		Irish Favourites		Soup plus	
Biscuits, Brownies & Bisotti		Italian Favourites		Spanish Favourites	
Bites		Jams & Jellies		Stir-fries	
Bowl Food		Japanese Favourites		Stir-fry Favourites	
Burgers, Rösti & Fritters		Kebabs & Skewers		Summer Salads	
Cafe Cakes		Kids Party Food		Tagines & Couscous	
Cafe Food		Lebanese Cooking		Tapas, Antipasto & Mezze	
Casseroles & Curries		Low-Fat Delicious		Tarts	
Char-grills & Barbecues		Low Fat Fast		Tex-Mex	
Cheesecakes, Pavlova & Trifles		Malaysian Favourites		Thai Favourites	
Chinese Favourites		Mince Favourites		The Fast Egg	
Chocolate Cakes		Microwave		The Young Chef	
Crumbles & Bakes		Muffins		Vegetarian	
Cupcakes & Cookies		Noodles & Stir-fries		Vegie Main Meals	
Dips & Dippers		Old-Fashioned Desserts		Vietnamese Favourites	
Dried Fruit & Nuts		Outdoor Eating		Wok	
Drinks		Packed Lunch			
Easy Pies & Pastries		Party Food			
Fast Fillets		Pickles and Chutneys			
Fishcakes & Crispybakes		Pasta			
Gluten-free Cooking		Potatoes		TOTAL COST £	

Photocopy and complete coupon below

Name _____

Address _____

_____ Postcode _____

Country _____ Phone (business hours) _____

Email*(optional) _____

* By including your email address, you consent to receipt of any email regarding this magazine, and other emails which inform you of ACP's other publications, products, services and events, and to promote third party goods and services you may be interested in.

I enclose my cheque/money order for £ _____ or please charge £ _____ to my:

☐ Access ☐ Mastercard ☐ Visa ☐ Diners Club

Card number

3 digit security code *(found on reverse of card)* _____

Cardholder's signature _____ Expiry date ____ /____

To order: Mail or fax – photocopy or complete the order form above, and send your credit card details or cheque payable to: Australian Consolidated Press (UK), 10 Scirocco Close, Moulton Park Office Village, Northampton NN3 6AP, phone (+44) (01) 604 642200, fax (+44) (01) 604 642300, e-mail books@acpuk.com or order online at www.acpuk.com

Non-UK residents: We accept the credit cards listed on the coupon, or cheques, drafts or International Money Orders payable in sterling and drawn on a UK bank. Credit card charges are at the exchange rate current at the time of payment. All pricing current at time of going to press and subject to change/availability.

Postage and packing UK: Add £1.00 per order plus 75p per book.

Postage and packing overseas: Add £2.00 per order plus £1.50 per book. **Offer ends 31.12.2009**